TRACES OF INK
Robert Pinget

*Translated and with an Afterword
by Barbara Wright*

Red Dust New York 2000

Pinget titles, translated by Barbara Wright
and published by Red Dust.

The Libera Me Domine   1978
Passacaglia   1978
Fable 1980
Between Fantoine and Agapa, 1982,
That Voice   1982
Someone   1984
The Apocrypha 1986
Abel and Bela 1987
Monsieur Songe (containing Monsieur Songe, The Harness and Plough) 1989
A Bizarre Will (plays) 1989
The Enemy 1991
Be Brave 1994
Theo or the New Era 1994
Traces of Ink   2000

Traces of Ink by Robert Pinget was originally published as *Taches d'Encre* by Les Éditions de Minuit in 1997.

Taches d'Encre copyright © Les Éditions de Minuit 1997

Copyright © this translation Barbara Wright 2000

ISBN 0-87376-089-1

Published in the United States of America by Red Dust, Inc.

All rights reserved

FOREWORD

This little book is Monsieur Songe's last notebook. He reveals himself frankly in it as naive, weary of fine phrases, and not bothered about contradicting or repeating himself. Perhaps he should have kept these pages to himself, but the need to share his uncertainties prevailed. May he be forgiven one last time.

RP

Find out who is making these notes.

Monsieur Songe

I

Continuation or end. New nightmare. No other way to keep yourself company.

Find out who is making these notes.

A leap into the elsewhere, the breathable.

An open door. You daren't believe it.

Fragments. Plethora. Remains. Bring dreams into these leftovers.

Or the impossible.

Alone on his morning walk Monsieur Songe says I'm old, full of care, I'm losing my head. I need a servant now.

And he starts looking at every street corner.

•

Being inclined to sleep too much, quite late after dinner he makes an effort and goes out into the garden to take the air, sitting on the bench with his cats, creatures of the night.

•

If one knew the password between one night and the next perhaps one would refuse to sleep.

•

And why be afraid of that password? All Monsieur Songe has ever liked is to go to bed.

•

Find out who is making these notes.
But only get to know him later, from a chance word on the page.

•

Disperse the shadows by blackening the dream.
Obscurum per obscurius.
That alchemy which so fascinated us.
Already passed into the experience of our daily death?

•

Repeat until loss of breath. The only lesson from the years of work.

•

Bow your head before the images evoked.
They are braver than the image-maker.

•

A corpse is concealed in the library.
Don't look for it. It's a memory.

•

Don't be afraid of going beyond logic, it will always catch you up in the end.

•

Rediscover that word which when repeated stood for everything.

•

To appreciate someone think of his capacity for admiration.

•

Happiness precedes the time when you tell yourself you are happy.

•

Let us no longer aim at being amusing or touching, but bear witness to those moments when we lose our heads.

•

Voices all around.
Not enough ears, not enough love.

•

What is needed or would have been needed...
Continue. No longer know who is talking.
Secret ear as a guide. Voices mixed up.
Re-emerge into the paradise of the game. Of the wager. Of chance.

•

What to do against fatigue?
Exhaust yourself.

•

Plunge into the irrational to try to reach the unconscious, the source of all poetry.
What other aim is conceivable?

•

To win people's favour say a few kind words that you don't mean.
Safeguard of solitude.

•

The time spent in meditation is of a different order from everyday time. It can't be counted.

•

Summer has come. The heart hasn't followed it. It's awaiting the liberating word.

•

Pen, slave driven by the hand, the servant of the voice.
Supreme ear.

•

This pen that makes us formulate what we don't know.
Will it suffice to reveal the secret?
Wait for the surprise.

•

Monsieur Songe discovers that the best way to be alive is to say so.
Very personal discovery.

•

By playing with words you venture towards the impossible.
Don't try to be original. The impossible is common currency for every gambler.
Sit down at your work table and say I want to be banal.

•

He listened to his heart beating for no reason.
A slight temperature.

•

No longer recognize yourself in the mirror. A fine lesson day after day.

•

Night. Night again.
What does it bring you?
Its long vowel.
Repeat night, night.

•

Torment of writing, torment of not writing.
Torment of sleeping, torment of not sleeping.
Torment of dying...

•

Say something, it doesn't matter what but say it, a Good Fairy murmurs.
The Wicked Fairy cackles.
How can a deaf man tell the difference between them?

•

If noise were a muse there would be so much poetry nowadays.
But too much noise...

•

If you ask yourself about poetry, what it is, where it comes from, you get no answer.
It's beyond all reasoning.
Banal.

•

Don't try to fathom enigmas. Secrets have their *raison d'être*.

•

To know the hour of our death would be to deprive ourselves of our power of imagination.

•

I want to get out of this room it's my death chamber says Monsieur Songe.

He dresses, puts on his shoes, goes downstairs and out of the front door into the street where he gets run over by a drunken motorcyclist.

Should they block the streets or ban the sale of motorbikes or lock up drunkards?

A question of life and death. Which you can't solve without risking the madhouse.

•

The instantaneous is what has not yet had time to die.

It's a snapshot which you collect and keep in an album with other photographs.

•

To what do I owe the honour of your visit?

The flowers brought by the visitor turn into a blood-red gruel.

•

Night only frightens those who have no shadow.

•

The only drama that touches him now is that maintained by silence.

•

An unknown force.

Wait for it hope for it create it simply by saying unknown force.

•

Accept your solitude and rid yourself of the idea of guilt.

•

A great poet said that if you want to write you have to be bored.

But he added that your boredom must be of good quality.

•

He questioned the Sibyl to find out what she couldn't tell him.

•

Why this daily exercise, such painful labour?

So as not to get out of the habit of not knowing how to write.

•

Repeat the dream. Repeat overcome. Repeat unknown force.

Repeat, so as to forget the nightmare of silence and to keep yourself company in a modest way.

•

Read great books to comfort yourself. Let beautiful images take shape behind your eyes without intervening.

Confidence will come.

•

His sense of justice urges him to be generous to the poor. But thinking over this expenditure later he considers it excessive.

And so regrets his generosity which he can only describe as concealed avarice.

•

His guardian angel says I would like a luminous shirt. Some people can't see me in my grey shirt and they can't get any light on themselves.

•

It took him longer to cross out what he'd written than to write it.

But even longer to regret what he'd said than to say it.

•

The grand organ of the night.

•

It's bright sunlight and not night that represents death. Sunlight kills. Night gives birth.

•

His friend Mortin says at the end of our days we ought to be able to say or write a phrase that would sum up our whole life, our joys, our hopes, our disillusionments.

He replies our disillusionments, yes. But that would make a lot of phrases.

•

A bit of courage, what the devil.

If it's the devil that gives courage we'll have to reconvert. But he claims to be legion.

•

The supernatural—an integral part of a natural state.

The potential miracle will always be there.

•

We might like to spend our whole time sleeping in order to dream, but it's the waking dream that makes us grow.

•

You mustn't feel any obligation.

A vulgar expression.

What is there that is not an obligation, even our pleasures.

•

To do things for ourselves—wouldn't that be to the detriment of other people?

•

What is said may have unconscious springs or motivations.

The trouble is that springs break and things said go off the rails.

Whence misunderstandings and dramas.

•

A beloved person once said to him when someone bores you, try and see him with a different eye. You may find it works.

•

When a tiresome fellow is shocked by the contradictions in his writings Monsieur Songe advises him to read them backwards.

•

To forget your own nothingness concentrate on that of someone else.

•

Sad awakening. Through the slit in the shutter, light has killed the night.

•

Rather than keep on saying the light is killing me why don't you move down into your cellar Mortin asks him.

He replies there will always be too much light somewhere.

Mortin doesn't retort poor old fellow the cemetery isn't far away.

•

How can it be that you are two people when you are the only one writing?
Banal.

•

One word plus one word can make a phrase but what good is that if your heart isn't in it?
Or else.
Try and write your phrases without putting your heart in them, it will find its way there.

•

The first beautiful spring day.
Instead of delighting in it he is plagued by a nasty thought.
Someone has shown a lack of respect for him and it made him furious.
Respect is a big word. Friendship would be better.
More precious than a beautiful day.

•

My dear mystic, he said to someone, you have nothing to worry about, if you keep on burning you'll end up in ashes.

•

None of this gets off the ground though.

The morning angel remains silent, the midday one talks too much.

Wait for the evening angel

And then fall asleep.

•

You say that silence is the weapon of the devil. But does the devil exist, my dear Monsieur?

Yes, judging by your mug.

•

It would be funny if through writing so much bosh this hand were to rebel and the pen were to jump up and hit you in the face.

•

Monsieur Songe has abandoned all pretension to literature and one day he realizes that nothing interests him any more. He only cheers up when the sun begins to go down in the late afternoon.

So all he should write in his notebook is the colour of the sky, the shape of the clouds, and the time for him to go to bed.

•

Don't despair, my dear friend. If you keep on dying your childhood will be reborn.

Even if some people laugh at you.

•

Take care. If you beat your breast so hard you'll end up being guilty.

•

In his thoughts, an artist spontaneously translates everything he sees and hears into a possible exaltation of his art.

•

What logic can you draw inspiration from in order not to have any?

•

We were alone at table. Suddenly there's someone with us.

He speaks very softly. The moon only lights up a moth on his ear.

The evening will end in sadness without a burst of laughter from the visitor, who disappears.

•

If this flower wasn't on the table it would be in the meadow.

The Wicked Fairy cackles. Who tells you it's a flower?

Instantly, nothing remains on the table.

•

One day passes without concluding the previous one. What to do with the next?

•

According to one way of thinking it could be said that a work exists only through the observer's awareness of it.

•

The only future is in the idea we have of the past.

•

He loses the thread of his argument but persists in listening to what is getting written.

Find out who is making these notes.

•

Full of courage Monsieur Songe takes his walking stick, his haversack, his hat, and launches an assault on the mountain.

But the mountain retreats with every step he takes.

When suddenly he is no longer dreaming.

•

Make your way very gradually towards the pandemonium of unreason.

•

He says to a sparrow, I am as light as you and I want to fly over this swamp I am being sucked down into. Take me with you.

But one doesn't speak to a bird.

•

To say I have no more illusions means I still have some unforgettable ones.

•

About that servant business Mortin says, losing your head losing your head is that any reason to go looking for a servant at every street corner? Why not look in all the dustbins? If you go on like that *I* shall become the servant and keep you on a leash during our walks.

•

In the old days Monsieur Songe put everything he knew into his memoirs. When he rereads them he doesn't remember any of it. This is probably because he didn't know a great deal. Otherwise a few bits and pieces would have remained with him

•

Looking out of the window and counting the raindrops falling from the eaves is as good an occupation as any other provided they don't come down in buckets.

On some days that's what he's reduced to by our horrid climate.

•

You'd do better to watch your repetitions, some of them are exasperating.

•

    Going out shopping every day is only pleasant if he meets a friend and spends the morning with him sipping white wine on a café terrace.

    Eating noodles that evening, he will curse his friend.

II

Only great hearts become greater with age.
Petty ones become more petty.

•

Always better to say we than to say I.

•

You have to have said a lot to earn the right to say nothing.

•

Blind in one eye, with a wooden leg, leave your home and go off singing towards less sombre skies.

•

Repeat your phrases to the night.
It will know how to throw light on them.

•

Someone invisible is moving around in the empty house and leaving a tiny drop of blood on every piece of furniture.
You can hear him muttering great joy has departed and will never return.

•

Still no one.

Only a spider.

She spins an immense web, from one room to the next, in which the images of the former inhabitants get caught.

Someone comes into the house.

Horror of those faces hanging everywhere.

•

Someone says the sunlight doesn't come into my room any more.

A bat makes itself at home there.

Then a hundred.

Sleep out in the open under the stars.

•

Silence has adopted the shape of an owl.

It keeps an eye on the neighbourhood through a dormer window.

Its nest in the big room is full of droppings.

•

Nothing alive left in the house.

Grow hemlock there.

And prepare the flask for the brew.

•

Write some vague threat on the front door.
Neither simpletons nor children can read.

•

Shadows no longer provide shelter.
The guilty will be exposed to the sun until they are dead.

•

A hellish sky to temper the night of suffering.
A paradisal sky to darken the Eden of sensualists.

•

Suddenly, the storm.
Struck by lightning, a head goes rolling over in the debris.
Mute deserts. Silence.

•

Here, Monsieur Songe says something. But his voice has grown weaker.
Just a murmur can be heard. But not understood.

•

What a lot of dead people around us.
Perhaps why Monsieur Songe speaks so softly.
He'll fall silent when he's finished counting his dead.

•

Sleep, to forget the awakening.
A favour not granted him.

•

Repeat, who is making these notes.
This pen and another one, far away.
Who will talk about the faraway one?
The pen itself, but without saying so.

•

Can one speak without saying anything?
Certainly. It all depends on who is listening.

•

What will his phrase be today?
Let his pen answer for him. He would like to be absent from what he writes.
Too bad if his phrase remains his question.

•

A vine gets entangled in a washing line.
It will produce dried fruit.

•

Just when the swallows are gathering before they hibernate a good genie reverses the calendar.
And the swallows don't go.

•

Mystery only appeals to intelligent or warm-hearted people.

•

Enchantment.
A nightingale enchanted a sorceress.
Fearing the bird's power, she strangles the poor little thing.

•

The Wicked Fairy wants to turn the sky-blue of the chicory flower into blood-red to spite anyone who goes near it.

But the angel watches, and the poet admires.

•

We must waste no time in harvesting the grapes for fear of the werewolf says Monsieur Songe.

He reads bad books in the evenings.

•

Read something difficult to gain access to what is most personal, most secret in us.

In other words, start the machine with a fuel that comes from elsewhere.

•

It sometimes happens that Monsieur Songe doesn't understand everything he says.

He leaves this job to others, hoping they'll find as little nonsense as possible.

•

Words have a life independent of our reason.

Playing with them we discover a strange world—which is nevertheless our own.

•

Our only hope is to reconcile our conscience with our unconscious.

Difficult, in so far as a narrow conscience is a bad judge of unconscious effects.

•

We only analyze our feelings when they are losing their strength.

A grand passion is experienced without soul-searching. It's its decline that invites reflection.

•

This pen believes it can fool everyone by not naming the person who wields it.

•

I wouldn't give much for your notes, says Mortin, if they are only the result of boredom or despair, which is what you never stop saying. Find something else to justify them.

To which the other has no answer.

•

To try to remedy his inconsistencies Monsieur Songe insists on his deliberate contradictions.

Whom is he trying to fool?

•

Long-awaited night, beneficent night.

What wretch has never wished to prolong the hours of night, and of his sleep?

The Grim Reaper will grant his wish.

•

Dispossessed of himself through lack of concern for other people.

•

However defiantly you overuse the word death you'll still end up being unable either to pronounce or write it.

•

Repeat waking dream.

Our love of words guides us although we don't know their meaning. And dreams take their own shape, freed from our common sense.

This is when we have an intuition of the secret that makes us write.

•

Monsieur Songe believes he can be thought erudite if he cites here and there in his notes a few words by authors he has only half read.

•

Alone in the evening in the bistro on the corner, he drinks his glass of red and imagines a different future. What can he do to live better? Sell the house? Go off to the Marquesas? Hang himself in the loft?

And he has another glass.

And the next day ditto.

•

Your black devils bore me, says Mortin. If you don't know what to do to live better, stop asking yourself. That will present an occasion for you to please me.

•

He seems to remember having been this or that…
But he had perhaps simply been ill-adapted to his nature.

•

Is he right to set such store by his repetitions? Are they appropriate?

Where can he find another head that will go on writing?

His pen replies for him that it has no head, only a sort of neck.

•

Noting down what happens to you every day is not the kind of writing he appreciates.

Note down what doesn't happen?

•

A nasty shadow enters the bedroom, imitating the night.

Be afraid it might engulf the dream.

•

Among your notes there are two or three you wrote without thinking.

Are they enough to redeem the whole?

•

Too much sleep distorts the image of the next day.

Sleep no more.

•

The bird perching on the plum tree won't chirp until you come.

Don't be too long.

•

Don Quixote came out of his book to hear it read to him. Poets who know this never lack inspiration.

•

The fact that there is no answer to some questions ought to multiply the number of happy people.

•

The mediocrity of your notes doesn't validate the effort you put into making them.

I have already explained myself as best I could.

As worst, you mean, my dear friend.

•

When the two persons conducting this dialogue merge into one there will be silence for all time.

•

Monsieur Songe would prefer not to end his days in smug tranquillity.

He would like to find himself in a waking dream, that sweet folly he has been yearning for all his life but which demands daily, unsettling tension, for he is weak-willed and enjoys his comforts.

•

A door opens.

Monsieur Songe goes into a dark corridor. He strikes a match, and lights a candle he finds in his pocket.

The walls in the corridor are covered with death's heads.

A crack.

A death's head has just fallen.

He picks it up and hangs it on the nail in the wall.

•

In the room he's just come into he finds Mortin asleep in an armchair.

He goes up to him and shakes him. What are you doing there?

Mortin says I'm waiting for the rats of memory.

•

Another crack.

I am your dream, you poor old man, but you don't appear in it. Someone who isn't you gives me orders and suggests the images that you think you discovered.

•

It wasn't Mortin who was asleep in the armchair but Monsieur Songe himself.

Someone says he's waking from another sleep, the sleep of death.

For death is in him, more alive than his dream.

•

That someone who is listening.

•

It's getting later. Nearly sundown.
Things don't look so black to Monsieur Songe when night approaches.

•

A change of air a change of air.
Breathe the air of childhood. The sweet folly so yearned for will be found there.

•

To be enigmatic is to respect the unsayable.

•

The Wicked Fairy cackles. Monsieur wants to play at being an author but he's forgetting me. I shall always be there to change his carriage into a pumpkin.

•

That other head which makes the best of everything, which dreams wide awake, which admires without reservation, may perhaps be tucked away in the cracked nut of Monsieur Songe who could never cope with his ordeals.
Has he still some hope of seeing that head reappear?

•

There's something lacking in the landscape, it's a merry eye.

•

Some people don't know how to express themselves either in joy or in sorrow.

They are thought insensitive, but that is a grave error.

•

Deafness.

I didn't hear what he said but he smiled at me so nicely that I said thank you.

•

No flowers, by request.

One in the eye for anyone who dreamed of them.

•

It seems as if with the passing of time the things we love leave us, just like people.

But it's we who are on our way out.

•

A hermit who never slept used to dictate his poems to his visitors.

They called him the angel of the mute.

Monsieur Songe decides to go and see him.

He adopts the most humble air he can and stands in front of him and says nothing.

The hermit looks at him and says right away I don't like your air of humility. I only dictate my poems to the genuinely humble. Go home and pray to the angel of the mute, I am merely his representative. He will visit you himself on condition that he finds you defenceless.

•

If you try too hard to discover the meaning of what you say, you deprive yourself of a little poetry.

•

He had decided to stop judging people but he still does. Allow your judgment to whisper but don't listen to it.

•

What would Monsieur Songe do without Mortin's responses?
He would make them for himself but without conviction.

•

Monsieur Songe once again wonders why he speaks of himself in the third person.
It's the result of an error of judgment. The fear of revealing too much of himself by using I although in fact it's a better disguise than he.

•

An infernal machine, X- Y- Z- or whatever rays, which would enable us to see death keeping watch over every one of us.

No need for an infernal machine. It's enough to pass the same person in the street for forty years.

•

Having thought too much about it, So-and-So no longer believes in mystery.

Odd that he can pride himself on it.

•

He catches himself saying for some years now I've gone down a lot in my own estimation.

•

A chill prevents him from going out so he feels duty bound to walk up and down in his room following a well-established route. From the bed to the door, from the door to the bookshelf, from the bookshelf to the window, and this ten times a day.

But as the room is only twenty metres square, he bumps into everything and falls over every time.

III

Over the years a void has formed around me, my dear Mortin. The proof is that I have no one left to talk to but you.

No offence meant.

•

He reproaches himself for going on writing about himself in this notebook when he has already done so such a lot in the previous ones.

The fable he had woven around himself is today overstepping the limits he had set for it.

•

The beautiful, long-awaited image refuses to appear.

The Wicked Fairy is secretly preparing an image for the timorous that will make them shiver. A volcano underneath a glacier.

•

Follow your dream and despise any attempt to represent the real. At the risk of ridicule.

The sublime can only result from an adventurous decision.

See Don Quixote.

•

Mortin says, the touching side of your perseverance is that it obliges us to be aware of how petty we can be.

And he adds, taking your self-criticism as your subject is praiseworthy in that it implies a certain ideal.

To which Monsieur Songe replies, my ideal is likely to get lost in my continual criticism. And I'm afraid the long-awaited image is going to take on such proportions that only death can provide it. Although it won't be such a bad thing if it has the last word in my gibberish.

•

Monsieur Songe is thinking of founding a Black Devils' Club in his old age.

While waiting to find premises where they could meet and mope together, all the splenetic would be invited to get in touch with the founder and send him in writing a sentence so phrased that it would be impossible to know whether it was supposed to make you laugh or cry.

•

Werewolf.

In the nearby wood the foliage rustles at close of day.

Someone is there observing and listening to what is going on in the house.

The old man trembles but doesn't say a word. He switches on the outside light.

The foliage stops rustling.

•

Your only excuse for not remaining silent is the fear of letting death get a hold on you. But it's a vain fear because the Grim Reaper doesn't take the slightest notice of it. He propels silence into us no matter what our efforts.

To retain speech would be a pledge of eternity.

In their heart of hearts some people have faith in this pledge.

•

Some days not knowing the word melancholy would be enough to be able to ignore the word sadness.

But the word grief is unforgettable.

•

Magic figures, whether friendly or hostile, are waiting for an opportunity to appear and bear witness to the mystery that surrounds us.

Everyday routine stands in their way.

•

The Good Fairy they invited to their festivities sent them a hideous wood-louse to give them a distaste for their pleasure.

•

It had been such a long time since they'd seen him when Monsieur Songe went back to their village, Fantoine, with Mortin.

Extreme emotion at the sight of the few houses whose façades were unchanged, of the streets which seemed narrower, of the church with its blackened steeple.

Should they try to look up a few inhabitants? Ask at the post office which of them were still alive?

Hadn't the heart.

They left the Peugeot outside what used to be the Migeotte laundry, walked the three steps from the cobbler's to the Soulevert grocery, and then like cowards got back into their car and drove off towards the forest.

There, at least, there were no heartaches. The same beeches, the same elms, the same paths between the trees, the same rustling leaves.

To get over their disappointing initiative, a stop at the Sirancy bistro where a glass or two of red wine put them back on their feet.

You see, said Mortin, when I was talking about the rats of memory...

•

But those rats are hard to kill, and they don't bother about us.

Maybe have to see Agapa again, le Rouget, the grey hills...

May all the good genies—for there are some—grant that the filthy rodents be put to sleep and that our two friends may relive the blissful hours of their youth.

•

This morning he risked an outing to the new part of the town.

From a distance he admired the collegiate church and imagined the comings and goings of the inhabitants in the shopping streets. A feeling of nostalgia prevented him from crossing the bridge leading to the old city...

Brace himself a bit the next time.

•

Someone is listening.

So very attentively that you can hear him listening.

•

No vain rebellion. Let time pass and it will let you pass.

•

Visit to the zoo.

Watching the monkeys scratching themselves he hears some children behind him laughing. He turns around to laugh with them, the kids are pointing at his cap and he realizes he has put it on back to front.

•

Continuation of visit.

Monsieur Songe only watches the crowds of visitors.

•

Paying attention to what people say to us doesn't always imply consideration.

•

Bury yourself again in the books you used to read and no longer understand them.

Reread your marginal notes and get away with drawing a vague conclusion. What does it matter? The effort has been made and may well lead to unexpected consequences.

•

Reminiscences.

When he gets to the former Oublies crossroads Monsieur Songe can't find the rue Croquette. Oh come on, it was there, where the rue Whatsit crosses the other one what was it called again... Could their names have been changed too?

He looks for his glasses, can't find them, and addresses a passer-by. Could you tell me where rue Croquette is please?

The passer-by who is deaf says what?

Monsieur Songe says it again.

The man smirks and says don't worry they'll soon find it for you.

And Monsieur Songe suddenly remembers that the rue Croquette is where the funeral director's is. What had he been going to do there? He tries to remember, he can't. And then he does, he'd been looking for Clopette's, the baker's where they used to make such good cakes.

Poor head, poor old gourmand.

On his way home he goes down the wrong street and asks a passer-by...

Etcetera.

•

Some days the phrase he wants to write insists on starting with the word nothing.

Then he has to struggle with nothingness to be able to compose a more or less admissible whole.

•

To complain that joy has left you is a delusion.

Be glad that you can still deplore its absence.

It's when you don't suffer from it any more that you'll be ripe for the tomb.

•

Henceforth deprived of imagination he is tempted for his daily note to look back on some happy moments in the past. But so many precautions to avoid the rats...

He opens his heart to Mortin who says we did think about that, don't you remember, not so long ago you were talking about good genies in that connection. We must have confidence in them, we can't live in terror of the past, that would compromise what remains of our future.

•

Right, what shall I talk about then? You can see I'm trembling. The meals with my niece? She's certainly dropped me. Sosie's rabbit? The geraniums and hydrangeas in the garden? So many things forgotten, so much sadn...

Come on my friend, buck up, you're letting yourself go. Here, why don't you go over to the well and look...

•

There would have to be a surprise there, a pleasant discovery.

Monsieur Songe, who is already sweating at the idea of writing his note, can't find anything. The saving intention has been jeopardized.

Miserable rats, you really do exist.

•

When he rereads his text he stumbles at every word, judges it pointless and crosses it out.

The phrase gets reduced to a single line if it still survives.

•

Try all possible medicines, the only cure for some ills is the word.

•

In the evenings to keep himself company or to keep up to date he switches the TV on for the news. But as it bores him prodigiously he turns the sound down and goes into another room.

It gives him the illusion that he has a little company.

•

The poet has nothing but words with which to create magic. But they don't obey every conductor's baton. You can read a phrase composed of the rarest words and it will fall flat.

Reverse their order with a stroke of the pen and the phrase sparkles.

•

Yes, I know I said pen instead of baton, my dear friend.
My pen knows it and makes fun of me.
The time will come when I shall wring its neck it if dares make just one more blot.

•

An owl comes out at nightfall.
All the mystery of the garden awakens.
There are unknown shadows, secret breaths.
Life at that hour.

•

To pretend that adventure makes you live more intensely is simplistic.
Look at ascetics and hermits.

•

You've been telling me for so long, my dear friend, that you only come to life again at six in the evening, but you could at least be good company after that time, take some notice of me, stay up later... But you go to bed at ten. Four hours of life—is that normal? Mind you, I'm not saying this for myself...

Monsieur Songe doesn't know what to answer. And then he reacts.

My dear fellow, since we've been friends for so long you ought to know by now that it's nothing to do with you and that it's my own fatigue that fatigues me. *My* fatigue. Your turn will come, don't worry. And *you* won't be able to do anything about it either... Hm, I'm going to bed.

•

It's no use denying it, Mortin repeats, you are writing your diary. What's original about it is that you bring me into it here and there without even asking me. It's just too bad if you make me talk nonsense, that goes with all the rest.

•

If your niece has dropped you it's your own fault. How can you expect the woman to take the initiative and come and see her old grouch? If you're fond of her it's up to you to invite her.

And what your notes also lack is anyone other than you and me. In the old days you had your maid and you let her speak, she was amusing, your great-nephew Théo, the gardener, the neighbours, a whole lot of people who livened up your memoirs. You say you don't remember anything but it's not true, just a little effort would be enough to being all that lot back to life and stop boring yourself with your moral philosophy.

•

All that lot as you call them used to turn up under my pen without any effort, it was a pleasure to evoke them. My imagination is a thing of the past and my pen, whatever I may have said about it offhand, used to obey it. I didn't have to wring its neck. That's all there is to it.

•

Mortin isn't convinced. He repeats a little effort a little effort, it bores you I know but you'd be the first to benefit from it.

As for the rats they only attack memories that hurt.

•

When he says that he no longer believes in his memories, his life's work, all the response he gets is you old humbug, your vanity exceeds all bounds.

•

Better to depend on other peoples's vexations than on your own. One doesn't easily pardon oneself.

•

I let you come out with your drivel. But it distresses me. Where can I find you a reason to write something powerful? I'm racking my brains.

I'm not racking mine. To comment on great literature would be one reason but it tires me. I'm going to let the memory of it ripen. Come what may.

•

And your Black Devils' Club, what's become of that?

I'm thinking about it I'm thinking about it but I don't know how to organize it.

Splenetics have no initiative, the very most they'll do is phone but they won't put themselves out. It needs a touch of humour to get them together but I haven't any left. Could you help me? For instance, to draft a circular that wouldn't shock anyone, they're usually so sensitive, inviting them here first... Although, whom do we send the circular to?

To our few friends at first, they're all more or less depressives and that would make it snowball, they'd talk about it to their friends and you'd soon have a houseful until you find suitable premises. Yes, I'll certainly help you but I do ask you to make a little effort.

How?

By pretending not to be depressed any more. Hm, since it's the first of the month today we could start the letter with April Fool to make it amusing... And continue it with childish reflections on death being merely a completely generalized menace, not especially destined for depressives...

Childish reflections on death, easy to say but that's not my style.

It'll have to become your style if you're keen on your project. On the other hand, no, the circular isn't ideal after all. Phone, like everyone else, and you'll see.

Starting with April Fool?

•

    I can't seem to see what courage is any more.

    Now what are you on about?

    Can you congratulate someone on being courageous? Isn't it rather a question of temperament which he can do nothing about? To say I congratulate you on having such a temperament is the equivalent of congratulating him on having a nose of a particular shape. In any case nobody can acquire courage. You have it or you don't. There will always be the courageous and the timorous. Congratulations, then? Simply say I like your courage, I like your nose? Come on, answer me, say something.

    I don't like your nose.

•

    Rather than trying so hard to understand the incomprehensible we ought to do our best to invent something incomprehensible in everything that is blindingly obvious. We'd have some surprises.

    Examples.

•

    Repeat the alchemical formula *obscurum per obscurius*.

    Surround ourselves with the greatest possible mystery and express ourselves in the most obscure language so that our thought escapes everyone, as it escapes ourselves.

    This lesson from the great alchemists would take us beyond our deadly everyday life. But what a lot of wisdom we need to get to that point.

•

I found a phrase about the spring but it vanished with the cold and greyness... A malaise that breaks my heart.

Really my dear fellow, what you need is a good hiding. And stop pestering me with your heart.

•

Find a way to avoid the sadness lying in wait for him at every turn.

There are magic words for that but they change from one day to another. Sometimes the word joy is useless.

A certain drunkard tells him trink. But that word is not in his vocabulary.

•

Are you counting the years you still have to live?

I... yes... I... no.

•

He was following a funeral but didn't know whether it was his own.

Someone catches him by the sleeve. Yours or someone else's, what's the difference?

•

Some creators only progress through the feeling of failure.

They advance according to a backwards mechanism.

•

Keeping a dried flower in an album is only touching if the flower comes back to life when the album is opened again.

•

The unforeseen is what we have always been waiting for without realizing it.

•

I no longer know how to continue my notes. My moral standards bore me to tears, so does our conversation.

Even so it's thanks to our bits of chat that you've been able to fill your notebook. Not that I flatter myself about that, for God's sake, it's all so insipid.

What, then?

Nothing, then. Or rather, change your interlocutor.

You aren't one. I invent three quarters of what you're supposed to say to me.

Your inventions... ye-ess... It's your style you ought to change. Write some poems...

A poet, me? Are you joking?

Ye-ess.

•

And so, half joking half serious, Mortin says actually your notebook, why don't you send it to a publisher, that would create a diversion in your existence.

Are you putting me on? Who would want to publish these unsalable bits and pieces? As for a diversion, it would be just the same as noting down my trifles. So you see.

•

However, a few days later, a letter to Monsieur Songe. We shall be delighted... etcetera.

What's the meaning of this? Did you get in touch with this publisher without telling me?

No, I swear I didn't. It's just chance, as donkeys say. Answer him right away.

Answer what?

A thousand thanks dear Monsieur, my notebook is yours.

•

And then the years pass.

Anxiety.

What can he do to overcome it?

One line plus one line. And keep going at all costs.

•

Day after day something very gradually dies in every one of us but often we only discover it long afterwards and then we are amazed at so many sudden changes.

He thinks again of the humility that a wise man advised him to cultivate before anything else.

But it is so difficult to achieve that he has to content himself with admiring it.

•

Evening is falling. The owl darts out of the hayloft. Is the night going to reveal its magic to us?

Monsieur Songe looks at his bed... No, buck up, let's go out with the cats.

He goes through the door, down the three steps, and sprains an ankle.

The Wicked Fairy cackles.

•

Optimism is just as uncertain as pessimism but it keeps you better company.

•

With time the quality of soul of our most loved dead becomes clearer, as if their absence dispels the veil they wore out of modesty when they were alive.

•

His neighbours gather their potatoes with the same care he takes in gathering his ideas.

•

    Whenever he is reproached for his lack of logic Monsieur Songe replies that it is entirely imaginary and considers himself quits.

•

    Wait for the evening owl, the bird of wisdom.
    There should be a morning one.

•

    Probably the only good thing in your notes is what is unsaid.
    A word here or there that makes us hope... something different from the continuation you are giving it.

•

    Are you going to let me end like that?

R.P.

AFTERWORD

Traces of Ink is Robert Pinget's last published book. It came out in the spring of 1997, and was followed that summer by a colloquium in Tours celebrating every aspect of his work; this was a happy, successful occasion which Pinget much enjoyed. Only a month later, though, he had a stroke and died.

Pinget's first book, *Between Fantoine and Agapa,* was published in 1951, and during that decade he became known as a member of the "Nouveau Roman" group attached to the publishing house Les Editions de Minuit. Other members of the group were Samuel Beckett, Nathalie Sarraute, Alain Robbe-Grillet, Claude Simon, Claude Ollier... Pinget said that while it was "an honour" to belong to it, he had no theory about the New Novel; he "followed his own path." So did the other members, in their own very different ways.

From the 1950s until his death, Robert Pinget wrote more than 30 books: novels, plays, "notebooks". All different, they nevertheless all express his lifelong concerns. Over and over again he has stressed the prime importance to him of the "tone" of a work. In a note to the 1972 Red Dust translation of his *The Libera me Domine*, Pinget wrote: "It seems to me that the interest of my work up to the present has been the quest for a tone of voice... It would be a mistake to consider me a partisan of any 'school of observation'. If we are thinking in terms of objectivity, the ear has equally tyrannical exigencies. And the tone varies from each of my books to the next. There will never be an end to my research in this field." And he adds: "It is not what can be "said" or "meant" that interests me, but "the way in which it is said."

But it would be another mistake if we were to interpret this statement simplistically and literally. What Pinget's works "say", and "mean", he has always insisted, comes to him directly from his "unshakeable confidence" in his unconscious—in the collective unconscious. He sees his methods as ways to "open the tap to the unconscious—let us say to the feelings. This work could not be more spontaneous. It is almost a sort of fully conscious automatic writing..."

Hence his distrust of what most of us think of as logic, his reliance on paradox and contradictions, the importance he attributes to repetitions or recurrences. In 1982, describing his working methods in a colloquium at New York University, he said that apart from his primordial research into the tone of each of his books and into the different tones of voice of each character, "my novels are constructed on the recurrence of themes and their variations." He listed the four different ways in which he used recurrence, one of which was "the pure and simple repetition of certain key-phrases or 'leitmotifs' throughout the book, which thus increase its resemblance to a musical composition."

"All art constantly aspires towards the condition of music", as Walter Pater said more than a hundred years ago, and Pinget, a true musician and talented cellist, always shared this belief. His inner ear was attuned to what it is perhaps permissible to call the music of the spheres. He saw that no art is closer to music than poetry, and said that the aim of a work of art "must be only one simple thing which, I think, is called poetry."

And his prose is indeed always poetic and, as a result of his intense concentration on its "tone", it is also always musical. It is designed to be "heard", to be read aloud. When actually heard, it is impossible to miss the harmony of its sounds and rhythms. This was particularly the case when he read it himself—very simply and without histrionics. On one occasion not so very long ago, in a New York bookstore he and I read passages from several of his books, alternately in French and in English. I can still remember the effect this had on the audience.

In 1982, *Monsieur Songe* was published in French. In his introduction to the English translation, Pinget wrote: "For some twenty years now I have been finding relaxation from my work in scribbling these stories about Monsieur Songe. To the original *Monsieur Songe* I recently added as a complement *The Harness,* and *Plough.* Here, revised and collected in one volume are all three books which, I repeat, are a "divertissement". Monsieur Songe can be seen as Monsieur Pinget's alter ego, and he figures in two of Pinget's subsequent books, *Be Brave,* and this present one (*Taches d' encre.*)

Pinget endows Monsieur Songe with his own preoccupations. In particular, there is the vital importance attached to the unconscious, hence: to dreams, contradictions, repetitions, nostalgia, intimations of death. And yet, interwoven with all these grave subjects, his invincible humour is never far away.

He was especially pleased when he realized that the younger generation was now taking an interest in his writings and beginning to understand them. He expressed these feelings to Madeleine Renouard in the book of her interviews with him published in 1993.* Here he attributes some of the interest of young people to the remarkable staging of *Monsieur Songe* by Jacques Seiler, which played to packed houses.

The word "Traces" could be seen as a reference to the ink drawings Pinget occasionally made in the margins of his manuscripts, and perhaps to the traces of himself which may be perceived between the lines. His lifelong concerns, which become more and more vivid with each successive Monsieur Songe book, are here (in *Traces of Ink*) condensed to the utmost. Free rein is given to self-doubts, particularly on the value of writing. Monsieur Songe asks himself: "Is it right to set such store by his repetitions? Are they appropriate?" "Why this daily exercise, such painful labour?" And then he gently mocks himself: "To try to remedy his inconsistencies Monsieur Songe insists on his deliberate contradictions. Whom is he trying to fool?" It is Monsieur Songe's rational mind, though, that provokes these doubts; he is more assured when he states that "Our love of words guides us although we don't know their meaning. And dreams take their own shape, freed from our common sense. This is when we have an intuition of the secret that makes us write."

Even when he was in his thirties, Pinget's books, like

Beckett's, showed extraordinary empathy with the feelings of old men and their preoccupation with their imminent death. In *Monsieur Songe,* in which Monsieur Songe (even twenty years ago) considers himself an old man, the idea of death is constantly present. And yet, by no means all his reflections on the subject are either negative or sad. Death is often seen as a new beginning. At the end of *Plough,* he amuses himself by imagining various deaths for himself. "Prostrated by an embolism......" "Drowned in the river where he was fishing for minnows..." "Run over by a truck on his house-bistro route... He isn't recognized at first. A boy says but it's Monsieur Songe, look at his galoshes."

Pinget may not have been familiar with the work of his kindred spirit, Samuel Butler, who wrote his own *Notebooks* towards the end of the nineteenth century, but he would certainly have been comforted by the similarity of their ideas. "He who is not forgotten is not dead," Butler wrote. And: "Whenever we push truth hard she runs to earth in contradiction in terms... An essential contradiction in terms meets us at the end of every enquiry."

Pinget helps us to stay alive and sustain our own enquiry.

---

* ROBERT PINGET A LA LETTRE Entretiens avec Madeleine Renouard, Belfond 1993